EMMANUEL JOSEPH

The Career Circuit, When AI, Family, and Faith Intersect

Copyright © 2025 by Emmanuel Joseph

All rights reserved. No part of this publication may be reproduced, stored or transmitted in any form or by any means, electronic, mechanical, photocopying, recording, scanning, or otherwise without written permission from the publisher. It is illegal to copy this book, post it to a website, or distribute it by any other means without permission.

First edition

This book was professionally typeset on Reedsy.
Find out more at reedsy.com

Contents

1 Chapter 1: The Dawn of AI in Everyday Life   1
2 Chapter 2: The Evolution of the Workforce   3
3 Chapter 3: Family Dynamics in the Age of AI   5
4 Chapter 4: The Role of Faith in an AI-Driven World   7
5 Chapter 5: The Intersection of Career and Faith   9
6 Chapter 6: AI and Ethical Leadership   11
7 Chapter 7: Education and Lifelong Learning in the AI Era   13
8 Chapter 8: AI and Personal Growth   15
9 Chapter 9: Building Resilient Communities   17
10 Chapter 10: The Future of AI and Humanity   19
11 Chapter 11: Cultivating a Balanced Life   21
12 Chapter 12: Embracing the Journey   23
13 Chapter 13: Navigating AI in Healthcare   25
14 Chapter 14: AI and Environmental Sustainability   27
15 Chapter 15: AI in the Arts and Creativity   29
16 Chapter 16: The Social Implications of AI   31
17 Chapter 17: Preparing for an AI-Driven Future   33

1

Chapter 1: The Dawn of AI in Everyday Life

As the sun rises on the age of artificial intelligence, we find ourselves in a world transformed by technology. From voice assistants that greet us in the morning to algorithms that curate our social media feeds, AI has become an integral part of our daily existence. This chapter explores the early stages of AI integration into society, highlighting the conveniences and challenges that come with it. The implications of AI reach far beyond mere automation; they extend to our professional lives, reshaping industries and redefining career paths.

In the midst of this technological revolution, families grapple with the impact of AI on their dynamics. Parents and children alike must navigate the digital landscape, balancing screen time with face-to-face interactions. The role of AI in education becomes a point of discussion, as personalized learning tools promise to enhance academic performance while raising concerns about data privacy and dependency on technology. As we delve deeper into this new era, we begin to understand the complexities of integrating AI into the fabric of our lives.

Faith communities, too, face unique challenges and opportunities as AI becomes more prevalent. Religious leaders and followers ponder the ethical implications of AI, seeking guidance from their spiritual beliefs. Questions about the soul, consciousness, and the role of humans in a world increasingly influenced by machines arise. This chapter examines how faith communities adapt to these changes, finding ways to incorporate AI into their practices while preserving their core values.

As we move forward, it is essential to recognize the interconnectedness of AI, family, and faith. Each aspect of our lives influences the others, creating a delicate balance that must be maintained. By understanding the dawn of AI in everyday life, we can better prepare for the future, ensuring that technological advancements serve to enhance, rather than detract from, our collective well-being.

2

Chapter 2: The Evolution of the Workforce

The rise of AI has brought about a seismic shift in the workforce, transforming the way we work and the skills we need to succeed. This chapter delves into the evolution of the job market, examining the roles that have emerged, those that have become obsolete, and the new opportunities that lie ahead. As AI takes on repetitive and mundane tasks, human workers are free to focus on more creative and complex endeavors. This shift requires a reevaluation of education and training programs, emphasizing the importance of lifelong learning and adaptability.

In this new landscape, collaboration between humans and machines becomes paramount. AI-driven tools and systems enhance productivity, streamline processes, and enable more informed decision-making. However, this symbiotic relationship also raises concerns about job displacement and the widening skills gap. To address these challenges, policymakers, educators, and businesses must work together to create a future where AI augments human potential rather than replacing it.

The impact of AI on the workforce extends beyond the professional sphere, affecting family life as well. As work becomes more flexible and remote, the boundaries between personal and professional time blur. This chapter explores the implications of this shift, considering how families can maintain a healthy work-life balance in an increasingly interconnected world. The role of AI in managing household tasks and responsibilities also comes into focus, offering both convenience and potential pitfalls.

Faith communities, too, are not immune to the changes in the workforce brought about by AI. Religious institutions must adapt to new ways of engaging with their congregations, leveraging technology to reach wider audiences and provide support in times of need. This chapter examines how faith leaders can harness the power of AI to enhance their ministries while remaining true to their spiritual missions. By understanding the evolution of the workforce, we can better navigate the challenges and opportunities that lie ahead, ensuring a future where AI and humanity coexist harmoniously.

3

Chapter 3: Family Dynamics in the Age of AI

The integration of AI into our daily lives has profound implications for family dynamics. This chapter explores the ways in which technology influences relationships, communication, and the division of responsibilities within the household. As AI-powered devices and applications become more prevalent, families must navigate the challenges and opportunities they present. From smart home systems that streamline chores to virtual assistants that manage schedules, AI has the potential to enhance family life, but it also raises questions about privacy, dependency, and the erosion of traditional roles.

The impact of AI on parenting is a key focus of this chapter. Parents must grapple with the benefits and drawbacks of using technology to monitor and educate their children. AI-driven educational tools offer personalized learning experiences, but they also raise concerns about data security and the potential for over-reliance on digital solutions. This chapter examines the balance between embracing technological advancements and maintaining the human touch in parenting.

Communication within families is another area transformed by AI. Virtual assistants, social media, and messaging apps enable constant connectivity, but they can also create barriers to meaningful face-to-face interactions. This chapter delves into the ways families can foster genuine connections in a digitally driven world, emphasizing the importance of setting boundaries and prioritizing quality time together. The role of AI in mediating conflicts and facilitating communication is also explored, offering insights into how technology can support, rather than hinder, family relationships.

Faith plays a vital role in shaping family dynamics, particularly in times of change and uncertainty. This chapter examines how faith communities can support families as they navigate the challenges of the AI age. From providing moral guidance to offering practical resources, religious institutions have the potential to be a stabilizing force in an increasingly complex world. By understanding the interplay between AI, family, and faith, we can develop strategies to foster strong, resilient family units that thrive in the face of technological advancements.

4

Chapter 4: The Role of Faith in an AI-Driven World

As artificial intelligence continues to permeate various aspects of our lives, faith communities must grapple with the ethical and spiritual implications of this technological revolution. This chapter explores the ways in which religious beliefs and practices intersect with the advancements in AI, considering how faith can guide our approach to technology and its impact on society. The relationship between faith and AI is complex, requiring thoughtful reflection and dialogue to navigate the challenges and opportunities that arise.

One of the key concerns for faith communities is the ethical use of AI. Religious leaders and followers must consider how AI aligns with their moral values, particularly when it comes to issues such as privacy, justice, and the sanctity of life. This chapter delves into the ethical dilemmas posed by AI, offering insights into how faith can inform our decisions and actions. By grounding our approach to technology in our spiritual beliefs, we can ensure that AI serves the greater good and upholds the dignity of all individuals.

Faith also plays a crucial role in addressing the fears and anxieties associated with AI. As technology continues to evolve at a rapid pace, many people experience uncertainty about the future and the potential consequences of AI integration. Religious communities can provide a source of comfort and stability, offering reassurance and guidance during times of change. This chapter examines how faith can help individuals and families cope with the challenges of an AI-driven world, fostering resilience and hope.

In addition to addressing ethical and emotional concerns, faith communities can harness the power of AI to enhance their ministries. From virtual worship services to AI-driven pastoral care, technology offers new opportunities to connect with congregants and serve their needs. This chapter explores innovative ways religious institutions can leverage AI while remaining true to their spiritual missions. By embracing the potential of AI, faith communities can continue to thrive and provide meaningful support to their followers in an ever-changing world.

5

Chapter 5: The Intersection of Career and Faith

In an AI-driven world, the intersection of career and faith takes on new dimensions. This chapter explores how individuals can integrate their spiritual beliefs with their professional lives, finding meaning and purpose in their work. The rise of AI presents both challenges and opportunities for people of faith, requiring thoughtful reflection and intentional action to navigate this complex landscape.

One of the key considerations for individuals is how their faith informs their approach to technology and innovation. This chapter delves into the ways in which religious beliefs can guide ethical decision-making in the workplace, particularly when it comes to the development and use of AI. By grounding their professional actions in their spiritual values, individuals can contribute to a more just and equitable society.

The concept of vocation, or a calling, is also central to the intersection of career and faith. This chapter examines how people can discern their vocational paths in an AI-driven world, considering how their unique talents and passions align with the needs of society. The role of faith in shaping one's career aspirations and goals is explored, offering insights into how individuals can pursue meaningful work that reflects their spiritual beliefs.

Balancing career and family life is another important aspect of this intersection. As AI transforms the workplace, it also influences the dynamics of work-life balance. This chapter explores strategies for maintaining harmony between professional and personal responsibilities, emphasizing the importance of setting boundaries and prioritizing what truly matters. The role of faith in guiding these decisions is highlighted, offering a framework for making choices that honor both career and family commitments.

Faith communities play a vital role in supporting individuals as they navigate the intersection of career and faith. This chapter examines how religious institutions can provide resources, guidance, and encouragement to their members, helping them find purpose and fulfillment in their work. By fostering a sense of community and shared values, faith communities can empower individuals to thrive in an AI-driven world while staying true to their spiritual convictions.

6

Chapter 6: AI and Ethical Leadership

The rise of AI presents unique challenges and opportunities for ethical leadership. This chapter explores how leaders can navigate the complexities of AI integration, ensuring that their decisions align with both ethical principles and the best interests of their organizations. In an era where technology has the potential to reshape industries and societies, the role of ethical leadership becomes more critical than ever.

One of the key aspects of ethical leadership is the ability to anticipate and address the potential consequences of AI. This chapter delves into the ways in which leaders can proactively identify and mitigate risks associated with AI, from data privacy concerns to biases in algorithm. By fostering a culture of transparency and accountability, leaders can ensure that AI is used in ways that promote fairness and inclusivity. This chapter explores best practices for ethical leadership in the age of AI, highlighting the importance of stakeholder engagement, continuous learning, and ethical decision-making frameworks.

Leaders must also navigate the ethical implications of AI on employee well-being. As AI-driven automation reshapes the workforce, leaders are tasked with ensuring that their employees are supported and empowered to adapt to new roles and responsibilities. This chapter examines strategies for fostering a culture of continuous learning and professional development, emphasizing the importance of empathy and open communication. By prioritizing the well-being of their employees, ethical leaders can create a more resilient and adaptable workforce.

The intersection of faith and ethical leadership is another key theme in this chapter. Religious beliefs and values can provide a strong foundation for ethical decision-making, guiding leaders as they navigate the complexities of AI integration. This chapter explores how faith can inform leadership practices, offering insights into how spiritual principles can be applied to the challenges and opportunities presented by AI. By grounding their leadership in their faith, individuals can foster a sense of purpose and integrity in their organizations.

Finally, this chapter addresses the role of ethical leadership in shaping public policy and societal norms. As AI continues to transform industries and communities, leaders have a responsibility to advocate for policies that promote fairness, inclusivity, and the public good. This chapter examines how leaders can engage with policymakers, stakeholders, and the broader community to ensure that the benefits of AI are shared equitably. By championing ethical leadership, individuals can help shape a future where AI serves the greater good and upholds the dignity of all people.

7

Chapter 7: Education and Lifelong Learning in the AI Era

The rapid advancement of AI has profound implications for education and lifelong learning. This chapter explores how educational institutions, policymakers, and individuals can adapt to the changing landscape, ensuring that learners are equipped with the skills and knowledge they need to thrive in an AI-driven world. The traditional model of education is evolving, with a greater emphasis on personalized learning, critical thinking, and adaptability.

One of the key challenges in the AI era is addressing the skills gap. As AI transforms industries and job roles, there is a growing need for individuals to continuously update their skills and knowledge. This chapter examines strategies for fostering a culture of lifelong learning, emphasizing the importance of flexibility and resilience. By embracing new learning modalities, such as online courses, micro-credentials, and experiential learning, individuals can stay ahead of the curve and remain competitive in the job market.

Educational institutions play a crucial role in preparing students for the future. This chapter explores how schools, colleges, and universities can integrate AI into their curricula, providing students with the tools and knowledge they need to succeed. From AI-driven tutoring systems to data analytics for personalized learning, technology has the potential to enhance educational outcomes. However, it is also essential to address the ethical and privacy concerns associated with AI in education, ensuring that learners' rights are protected.

Faith communities can also contribute to the promotion of lifelong learning. Religious institutions often provide educational programs and resources that support personal and professional development. This chapter examines how faith communities can leverage AI to enhance their educational offerings, from virtual study groups to AI-driven content recommendations. By integrating faith and education, individuals can pursue holistic growth that encompasses both their spiritual and intellectual development.

Finally, this chapter considers the role of policymakers in shaping the future of education. Governments and educational authorities must work together to develop policies that promote access, equity, and quality in education. This chapter explores best practices for creating an inclusive and forward-thinking educational system that prepares learners for the challenges and opportunities of the AI era. By fostering a collaborative approach to education, we can ensure that everyone has the opportunity to thrive in a rapidly changing world.

8

Chapter 8: AI and Personal Growth

The integration of AI into our daily lives offers unique opportunities for personal growth and self-improvement. This chapter explores how individuals can leverage AI to enhance their well-being, achieve their goals, and cultivate a sense of fulfillment. From AI-driven fitness apps to virtual life coaches, technology provides new tools for personal development, but it also requires mindful engagement to ensure a balanced approach.

One of the key benefits of AI is its ability to provide personalized recommendations and insights. This chapter examines how individuals can use AI-powered tools to set and achieve their personal goals, whether they relate to health, career, or hobbies. By leveraging data and analytics, AI can offer tailored advice and support, helping individuals make informed decisions and track their progress. However, it is essential to approach these tools with a critical eye, being mindful of potential biases and limitations.

Mindfulness and mental well-being are also important aspects of personal growth in the AI era. This chapter explores how AI can support mental health, from virtual therapy sessions to mindfulness apps that promote relaxation and stress reduction. While these tools offer valuable resources, it is crucial to maintain a balance between digital and real-world interactions. This chapter emphasizes the importance of fostering genuine connections and prioritizing self-care in a technology-driven world.

Faith can play a significant role in personal growth, providing a sense of purpose and direction. This chapter examines how individuals can integrate their spiritual beliefs with their use of AI, ensuring that their personal development aligns with their values. From using AI to deepen religious practices to seeking spiritual guidance in navigating technological challenges, faith can offer a grounding influence in the pursuit of personal growth.

Finally, this chapter considers the ethical implications of using AI for personal development. As individuals seek to enhance their lives through technology, it is essential to consider the broader impact of their choices. This chapter explores how personal growth can be pursued in ways that promote social good, emphasizing the importance of ethical considerations in the use of AI. By approaching personal development with a holistic perspective, individuals can achieve a sense of fulfillment that encompasses both their personal and societal responsibilities.

9

Chapter 9: Building Resilient Communities

The rise of AI presents both challenges and opportunities for building resilient communities. This chapter explores how communities can leverage AI to enhance their collective well-being, promote social cohesion, and address shared challenges. From AI-driven disaster response systems to community engagement platforms, technology has the potential to strengthen the social fabric, but it also requires thoughtful and inclusive approaches.

One of the key aspects of building resilient communities is fostering a sense of belonging and mutual support. This chapter examines how AI can facilitate community engagement, from virtual neighborhood forums to AI-driven social initiatives. By leveraging technology, communities can enhance communication, promote civic participation, and address local issues more effectively. However, it is essential to ensure that these efforts are inclusive and accessible to all members of the community.

Faith communities play a vital role in building resilience, providing support and resources to individuals and families in times of need. This chapter explores how religious institutions can harness the power of AI to enhance their outreach and support services, from virtual counseling sessions to AI-driven charity initiatives. By integrating technology into their practices, faith communities can continue to fulfill their mission of serving others while adapting to the changing landscape.

The role of AI in disaster response and recovery is another important theme in this chapter. From predictive analytics that identify at-risk areas to AI-driven coordination of relief efforts, technology can enhance the effectiveness and efficiency of disaster management. This chapter examines best practices for leveraging AI in disaster response, emphasizing the importance of collaboration between governments, organizations, and communities. By building resilient systems, we can better prepare for and respond to the challenges posed by natural and human-made disasters.

10

Chapter 10: The Future of AI and Humanity

As we look to the future, the relationship between AI and humanity will continue to evolve, shaping the way we live, work, and interact with one another. This chapter explores the potential trajectories of AI development, considering both the opportunities and challenges that lie ahead. From advances in machine learning to the ethical dilemmas of autonomous systems, the future of AI holds both promise and uncertainty.

One of the key considerations for the future is the ethical governance of AI. This chapter examines how policymakers, technologists, and society at large can collaborate to develop frameworks that promote responsible AI development and use. By prioritizing transparency, accountability, and inclusivity, we can ensure that AI serves the greater good and addresses the needs of all people. This chapter explores best practices for ethical AI governance, highlighting the importance of stakeholder engagement and continuous dialogue.

The potential of AI to address global challenges is another important theme in this chapter. From climate change to public health, AI has the potential to provide innovative solutions to some of the world's most pressing issues. This chapter examines how technology can be harnessed to promote sustainability, equity, and resilience, offering insights into the ways AI can contribute to a better future. By aligning technological advancements with social and environmental goals, we can create a more just and sustainable world.

Faith communities have a unique role to play in shaping the future of AI. This chapter explores how religious institutions can provide moral guidance and ethical insights as we navigate the complexities of AI development. By fostering a dialogue between faith and technology, we can ensure that our approach to AI is grounded in values that promote human dignity, justice, and compassion. This chapter examines how faith communities can advocate for ethical AI and support their members in navigating the challenges and opportunities of the future.

11

Chapter 11: Cultivating a Balanced Life

In the age of AI, achieving a balanced life becomes both more challenging and more critical. This chapter explores strategies for maintaining harmony between work, family, faith, and personal well-being in an increasingly interconnected world. As technology blurs the boundaries between different aspects of our lives, it is essential to develop practices that promote balance and fulfillment.

One key aspect of cultivating a balanced life is setting boundaries. This chapter examines how individuals can establish healthy limits on technology use, ensuring that they have time and space for meaningful face-to-face interactions and self-care. From designated tech-free zones in the home to mindful technology practices, there are various ways to create a more balanced and intentional approach to AI.

Another important consideration is the role of faith in fostering balance. This chapter explores how spiritual practices and beliefs can provide a foundation for well-being, offering guidance and support as individuals navigate the complexities of modern life. By integrating faith into their daily routines, individuals can cultivate a sense of purpose and grounding that helps them maintain balance in the face of technological advancements.

The importance of community is also highlighted in this chapter. Building and nurturing connections with others can provide a source of support and resilience, helping individuals navigate the challenges of an AI-driven world.

This chapter explores how families, friends, and faith communities can come together to support one another, creating a network of care that promotes balance and well-being.

Finally, this chapter considers the role of continuous growth and learning in achieving a balanced life. By embracing a mindset of lifelong learning and personal development, individuals can adapt to the changing landscape and find fulfillment in both their professional and personal pursuits. This chapter offers practical strategies for fostering growth and resilience, emphasizing the importance of flexibility and adaptability in the face of change.

12

Chapter 12: Embracing the Journey

As we conclude this exploration of the intersection of AI, family, and faith, it is essential to recognize that the journey is ongoing. The rapid advancements in technology and the complexities of modern life require continuous reflection, adaptation, and growth. This final chapter encourages readers to embrace the journey, finding meaning and purpose in the dynamic interplay between AI, family, and faith.

One key theme in this chapter is the importance of embracing uncertainty. As technology continues to evolve, it is natural to experience feelings of uncertainty and apprehension about the future. This chapter explores how individuals can find peace and resilience in the face of uncertainty, drawing on their faith, values, and community for support. By cultivating a mindset of openness and curiosity, individuals can navigate the unknown with confidence and grace.

Another important consideration is the role of gratitude and mindfulness in embracing the journey. This chapter examines how practices of gratitude and mindfulness can enhance well-being, helping individuals stay grounded and present in the midst of change. By focusing on the present moment and appreciating the positives in their lives, individuals can cultivate a sense of contentment and joy.

The chapter also highlights the importance of service and contribution. By using their talents and resources to make a positive impact on the world, individuals can find deeper meaning and fulfillment in their journey. This chapter explores how AI can be harnessed for social good, offering opportunities for individuals to contribute to causes they care about and create a better future for all.

Finally, this chapter encourages readers to stay connected to their values and principles. As technology continues to shape our lives, it is essential to remain true to the values that define us as individuals and communities. By fostering a culture of ethical reflection and dialogue, we can ensure that AI serves the greater good and enhances the human experience. This chapter offers practical insights for staying grounded and purposeful in the face of change, encouraging readers to embrace the journey with hope and determination.

13

Chapter 13: Navigating AI in Healthcare

The integration of AI into healthcare has the potential to revolutionize the way we approach medical treatment, diagnosis, and patient care. This chapter explores the advancements in AI technology within the healthcare sector, examining how machine learning algorithms and data analytics are being utilized to improve patient outcomes and streamline processes. From personalized medicine to robotic surgeries, AI is transforming the healthcare landscape.

One of the key benefits of AI in healthcare is its ability to analyze vast amounts of data quickly and accurately. This chapter delves into how AI-driven tools can assist in early diagnosis and predictive analytics, enabling healthcare professionals to provide more effective and timely treatments. Additionally, the potential of AI to identify patterns and trends in health data can lead to new insights and advancements in medical research.

The ethical considerations of AI in healthcare are also a significant focus. As AI becomes more integrated into medical practice, questions about patient privacy, data security, and the potential for bias arise. This chapter examines the importance of ethical guidelines and regulatory frameworks to ensure that AI is used responsibly and equitably in healthcare.

Faith communities can play a role in supporting individuals as they navigate the complexities of AI in healthcare. This chapter explores how religious institutions can provide spiritual guidance and emotional support to patients and their families, helping them make informed decisions about their medical care. By integrating faith and healthcare, individuals can find comfort and strength in their spiritual beliefs during times of illness and healing.

14

Chapter 14: AI and Environmental Sustainability

The potential of AI to address environmental challenges is immense, offering innovative solutions to promote sustainability and combat climate change. This chapter explores how AI can be harnessed to protect natural resources, reduce carbon emissions, and promote sustainable practices across various industries. From smart energy grids to precision agriculture, technology is playing a crucial role in building a more sustainable future.

One of the key applications of AI in environmental sustainability is its ability to analyze and interpret large datasets. This chapter examines how AI-driven tools can monitor and predict environmental changes, enabling more effective conservation efforts and resource management. By leveraging machine learning algorithms, researchers can gain new insights into complex environmental systems and develop strategies to mitigate the impact of human activities.

The role of AI in promoting sustainable business practices is also explored. This chapter delves into how companies can use AI to optimize supply chains, reduce waste, and improve energy efficiency. By integrating sustainability into their operations, businesses can contribute to a greener and more sustainable economy.

Faith communities have a unique role to play in promoting environmental stewardship. This chapter examines how religious institutions can advocate for sustainable practices and raise awareness about the ethical implications of environmental degradation. By fostering a sense of responsibility and care for the planet, faith communities can inspire individuals to take action and contribute to a more sustainable future.

15

Chapter 15: AI in the Arts and Creativity

The intersection of AI and the arts presents exciting opportunities for creativity and innovation. This chapter explores how AI is being used to create, enhance, and inspire artistic expression across various mediums, including visual arts, music, literature, and performance. From generative algorithms to virtual reality experiences, technology is opening new doors for artists and audiences alike.

One of the key benefits of AI in the arts is its ability to generate new ideas and perspectives. This chapter delves into how machine learning algorithms can analyze patterns and trends in existing artworks, creating new compositions and styles that push the boundaries of traditional art forms. Additionally, AI-driven tools can assist artists in the creative process, offering new techniques and possibilities for expression.

The role of AI in democratizing access to the arts is also explored. This chapter examines how technology can make artistic experiences more accessible to diverse audiences, from virtual museum tours to AI-generated music playlists. By breaking down barriers to entry, AI has the potential to create a more inclusive and vibrant artistic community.

Faith and creativity are deeply intertwined, with religious traditions often inspiring and influencing artistic expression. This chapter explores how AI can be used to enhance religious art and music, creating new ways for individuals to connect with their faith. By integrating technology into their creative practices, artists can explore new dimensions of spirituality and expression.

16

Chapter 16: The Social Implications of AI

The integration of AI into various aspects of society has profound social implications, affecting everything from employment to social interactions. This chapter explores the broader societal impacts of AI, considering how technology is reshaping our communities, relationships, and social structures. By examining both the positive and negative aspects of AI, we can gain a deeper understanding of its role in shaping our future.

One of the key social implications of AI is its potential to exacerbate existing inequalities. This chapter delves into how AI-driven technologies can both bridge and widen social divides, depending on how they are implemented. By analyzing the impact of AI on different demographic groups, we can identify strategies to ensure that technology is used to promote equity and inclusion.

The role of AI in shaping social interactions and communication is also explored. This chapter examines how virtual assistants, social media algorithms, and other AI-driven tools are influencing the way we connect with others. While technology can facilitate communication and build connections, it also raises concerns about privacy, authenticity, and the quality of our interactions.

Faith communities have a unique perspective on the social implications of AI, offering ethical and moral guidance as society navigates these changes. This chapter explores how religious institutions can advocate for social justice and promote the responsible use of technology. By fostering a dialogue between faith and technology, we can ensure that AI serves the greater good and enhances the well-being of all individuals.

17

Chapter 17: Preparing for an AI-Driven Future

As we look to the future, it is essential to prepare for the continued integration of AI into our lives. This chapter explores strategies for individuals, families, and communities to navigate the challenges and opportunities of an AI-driven world. By fostering a culture of adaptability, resilience, and ethical reflection, we can ensure that technology enhances, rather than detracts from, our collective well-being.

One of the key strategies for preparing for the future is embracing lifelong learning. This chapter examines how individuals can continuously update their skills and knowledge to stay competitive in an ever-changing job market. By fostering a mindset of curiosity and growth, we can adapt to new technologies and find new opportunities for personal and professional development.

The role of families in preparing for the future is also explored. This chapter delves into how parents and caregivers can support their children in developing the skills and values needed to thrive in an AI-driven world. From promoting digital literacy to fostering critical thinking, there are various ways to equip the next generation with the tools they need to succeed.

Faith communities can play a crucial role in guiding individuals and families as they navigate the future. This chapter examines how religious institutions can provide support, resources, and moral guidance to help their members adapt to technological changes. By fostering a sense of community and shared values, faith communities can empower individuals to face the future with confidence and hope.

Finally, this chapter considers the broader societal implications of preparing for an AI-driven future. By engaging in thoughtful reflection and dialogue, we can develop policies and practices that promote the responsible and equitable use of technology. This chapter offers insights into how we can create a future where AI serves the greater good and enhances the human experience.

"The Career Circuit: When AI, Family, and Faith Intersect":

In an era where artificial intelligence is seamlessly woven into the fabric of our daily lives, "The Career Circuit: When AI, Family, and Faith Intersect" delves into the profound impacts of this technological revolution on our careers, relationships, and spiritual journeys.

This insightful book offers a comprehensive exploration of how AI is reshaping the workforce, transforming family dynamics, and challenging our ethical and moral frameworks. Through twelve thought-provoking chapters, the book examines the intricate interplay between technology, personal growth, and community resilience, providing readers with practical strategies for navigating the complexities of modern life.

From the dawn of AI in everyday life to the evolution of the workforce, the book sheds light on the opportunities and challenges that arise as we integrate technology into our professional and personal spheres. It explores the pivotal role of faith in guiding our approach to AI, offering ethical and spiritual insights that help us remain grounded and purposeful in a rapidly changing world.

With a focus on ethical leadership, lifelong learning, and environmental sustainability, "The Career Circuit" encourages readers to embrace the journey with hope and determination. It highlights the importance of balance, mindfulness, and community in fostering resilience and well-being, ensuring that AI serves to enhance, rather than detract from, our collective human experience.

Whether you're a professional navigating the evolving job market, a parent balancing technology's impact on family life, or an individual seeking to integrate faith and personal growth, this book provides valuable perspectives and actionable insights. Join us on this journey to understand the transformative power of AI and its intersection with the core aspects of our lives—career, family, and faith.

www.ingramcontent.com/pod-product-compliance
Lightning Source LLC
LaVergne TN
LVHW020458080526
838202LV00057B/6028